Bibliographic information published by the German National Library:

The German National Library lists this publication in the National Bibliography; detailed bibliographic data are available on the Internet at http://dnb.dnb.de .

Imprint:

Copyright © 2006 GRIN Verlag, Open Publishing GmbH
Print and binding: Books on Demand GmbH, Norderstedt Germany
ISBN: 9783656734154

This book at GRIN:

http://www.grin.com/en/e-book/279757/advantages-and-disadvantages-of-oral-verbal-communication-and-written-communication

Teddy Kimathi

Advantages and Disadvantages of Oral/Verbal Communication and Written Communication

GRIN Publishing

GRIN - Your knowledge has value

Since its foundation in 1998, GRIN has specialized in publishing academic texts by students, college teachers and other academics as e-book and printed book. The website www.grin.com is an ideal platform for presenting term papers, final papers, scientific essays, dissertations and specialist books.

Visit us on the internet:

http://www.grin.com/

http://www.facebook.com/grincom

http://www.twitter.com/grin_com

ADVANTAGES AND DISADVANTAGES OF ORAL/VERBAL COMMUNICATION AND WRITTEN COMMUNICATION

BY

TEDDY KIMATHI

ADVANTAGES AND DISADVANTAGES OF ORAL/VERBAL COMMUNICATION AND WRITTEN COMMUNICATION.

Oral communication has several advantages and disadvantages, compared to written communication, which has several advantages too and a few disadvantages. When we look at the way these two types of communication, in relation to our day to day lives interrelate with each other, and then basic communication skills will be much more efficient and effective.

Looking first at the advantages and disadvantages of the oral communication, we will know more about it. For its good side, this kind of communication is less time consuming as compared to written communication. For instance, when the speaker is giving out the speech, he/she is able to answer the questions of audience freely and give great ideas. The speaker does not waste time referring to a particular book or text.

Secondly, the speaker and audience are closer to each other, in terms of individual personality and ideas. This is common in seminars, lectures and research meetings. As it is a direct communication process, the audience respects the speaker for he/she is the one who has the ideas and knowledge of a particular subject.

Thirdly, when we look at the world of entertainment, singers and actors are able to reach the hearts of the audience, due to the art they perform either through singing, dramatizing or giving a short speech. Just a few years ago, international artists organized a concert which was supposed to help people who were dying of hunger in Somalia and Ethiopia. By just singing about hunger and poverty, the concerts raised millions and millions of dollars which were used to buy food and medical equipment and medicines for the hungry.

Fourthly, when we look at the countryside and remote areas, people inhibiting these places have been able to get vital information through audio communication machines, the most common one being the radio. By just receiving news from such devices, the listeners get the picture or idea quickly of what is being talked of/about.

Verbal communication has negative aspects also. The first aspect concentrates on the confusion of the real and false in history and religion. Looking at religion, we will realize that the life story and upbringing of Jesus Christ and Muhammad some similarities reveal themselves. Today's Muslims will tell us that Muhammad's mother, Amina was visited by an angel called angel Gabriel. Looking at Christianity, Jesus' mother, Mary was visited too by the same angel. If it is not for the written texts or scriptures such s the Bible and Koran, these two religions would be at war.

For legends and stories about the lost kingdoms, empires and cities are told by grandparents and parents orally, an audience or listener is skeptical about the real existence of the ancient lands together with their last glory. Let us look at Greece, as a good example. Some Greek citizens claim that a city called Atlantis once existed. It had endless supply of gold, precious stones and food. Then one day it sank to the ground, never to be seen again. Without written scrolls, scripts or tablets supporting this fact, then it is very hard to prove of its existence to some people like literary scholars.

Oral communication, as a means of sending messages, is known of its notoriety in distorting or exaggerating a message or messages. Like in business, some businesses have collapsed because of giving the wrong information, either from superior to the sub-ordinates or from the sub-ordinates to the superior. Because of such dangerous mistakes, several businesses have opted to modern devices such as computers, telefax and fax to communicate. In social life, friends and families have become slaves of rumors, which have split their friendship and relationship to pieces without knowing the source or cause of the rumor.

Due to the same risky occupations such as the military, police and secrete service, this kind of communication has been limited in that area because of dangers like plugging of the listening devices or being overheard by the enemies. Just by looking at the cold war era, we will come to learn how the Soviet Union states suffered politically and socially because of their agents relying mainly on wired communication devices as a means of sending delicate information. On the side of military, some civil wars have also been received by careful spies and eavesdroppers.

Institutions like campuses, universities and colleges have difficulties in teaching and training students due to relying heavily on verbal communication. Because of this, lecturers and teachers who teach courses concentrating mainly on theory in form of speech realized that the only way to drive a point home from any of these courses is by using hands, heads and legs in expressing a reaction, rate, mood, size and even shape. As today's world becomes more sophisticate, verbal communication in training institutes is becoming confusing more and more , as materials for study and teaching increase.

Written communication has got advantages and disadvantages too. First we look at the advantages which affect people's minds, making them to opt for this kind of communication, rather than the oral communication. In the first point, intellectual classes of people have really benefited from this kind of communication by just going through a book, newspaper, journal or sheets of a paper printed by a computer, this kind of communication method has really helped readers to acquire more knowledge about a particular subject or situation.

The second factor is that is has expanded the horizon of education all over the world. With the availability of reading materials for all students and pupils in school, campuses and colleges, the effectiveness of learning has really improved in almost every part of world. Second world and third world countries have really benefited from this kind of learning skill, through written materials.

The other factor is that unlike in telecommunication and other modern forms of communication, written communication is much cheaper in terms of expenses. To send a message to someone living far away from his/her home, a person can just write a letter and take it to post office, where one is charged less. But modern machines such as the computers, telefax and fax have proved to be much more expensive.

Fourthly, as this kind of communication concerns the writing of information on various materials, the writing of information on various materials, the written information can be kept for future reference, especially in libraries. Unlike in oral communication where information is distorted or forgotten, the written information can't change its meaning or fade. Man has managed to unravel many ancient mysteries through the use of scrolls, tablets, scripts and booklets which show what really happened in a particular place with its date and name indicated. These materials have really helped us to learn and understand more about the historical Bible lands.

The last advantage is that concerning general facts, written communication is not exaggerated. Unlike in the oral traditions and customs where myths, fables and parables were used to convey a particular message in the past by ancestors, ancient libraries like the light house of Alexandria stored information, which was very important and fulfilling to the human race.

During that age, a historian or philosopher usually narrated his experience to a group of writers, who wrote the message they heard in scroll and scripts. If it was not for these libraries, we wouldn't know about the life story of great leaders, such as Alexander the Great and Ptolemy the first.

Even though written communication is supported by several advantages, it can't lack a few negative factors which make people's decision to be harder on judging the best communication method to use.

The first disadvantage is that if written information is not well stored or cared for, the information is lost or distorted. For example, if we look at the loss several libraries and archives have suffered, the number of vital information which vanished is unthinkable. In this modern world, fires have spread havoc in the shelves and cabinets which vital information.

Secondly, literates are the only people who can apply this kind of communication almost everywhere. Looking at illiterates, we will come to realize that reading materials such as newspapers or writing a letter and filling in a cash book is their major problem in this kind of communication, focusing on this situation we will notice that a boundary has been created separating literates from the illiterates.

Lastly, written communication is a slow method, if we look at the way people send letters to distant people. For instance, a letter from Nairobi to New York will possibly take days to arrive as compared to telephones, telefax and mobile phones, which take a few minutes to complete a conversation or message.

REFERENCE

Randall McCutchem, James Schaffer and Joseph R. Wycloff (1994). Communication Matters . West Publishing Company, United States of America.

Warren K. Agree, Philip H. Ault and Edwin Emery. New York (1988) Introduction to Mass Communication. Ninth Edition. Harper and Row, Publishers, United States of America.